Amazing Animal Defenses

Animals with
Wicked Weapons
Stingers, Barbs, and Quills

Susan K. Mitchell

Enslow Publishers, Inc.
40 Industrial Road
Box 398
Berkeley Heights, NJ 07922
USA

http://www.enslow.com

These books are dedicated to Emily, who inspired the author.

Library of Congress Cataloging-in-Publication Data
Mitchell, Susan K.
  Animals with wicked weapons : stingers, barbs, and quills / by Susan K. Mitchell.
      p. cm. — (Amazing animal defenses)
  Includes bibliographical references and index.
  Summary: "Readers will learn about the weapons that different animals have to protect themselves from predators"—Provided by publisher.
  ISBN 978-0-7660-3292-7
  1. Animal defenses—Juvenile literature. I. Title.
  QL759.M59 2009
  591.47—dc22

                                        2008011075

ISBN-10: 0-7660-3292-2

Printed in the United States of America

10 9 8 7 6 5 4 3 2 1

To Our Readers:
We have done our best to make sure all Internet Addresses in this book were active and appropriate when we went to press. However, the author and the publisher have no control over and assume no liability for the material available on those Internet sites or on other Web sites they may link to. Any comments or suggestions can be sent by e-mail to comments@enslow.com or to the address on the back cover.

♻ Enslow Publishers, Inc., is committed to printing our books on recycled paper. The paper in every book contains 10% to 30% post-consumer waste (PCW). The cover board on the outside of each book contains 100% PCW. Our goal is to do our part to help young people and the environment too!

Cover photo: Big Stock Photo/Steve Lovegrove
Interior photos: Alamy/Peter Arnold, Inc., pp. 6, 20; Alamy/Steve Bloom Images, p. 10; Alamy/PhotoAlto, p. 11; Alamy/Clearvista Photography, p. 13; Alamy/Mark Boulton, p. 14; Alamy/AfriPics.com, p. 17; Alamy/franzfoto.com, p. 18; Alamy/Bryan & Cherry Alexander Photography, p. 21; Alamy/Juniors Bildarchiv, pp. 22, 27; Alamy/Petra Wegner, p. 24; Alamy/Michael Sayles, p. 26; Alamy/blickwinkel, p. 27 (inset); Alamy/Brandon Cole Marine Photography, p. 33; Alamy/PhotoBliss, p. 34; Alamy/Auscape International Pty Ltd., p. 36; Alamy/John Cancalosi, p. 40; Animals Animals–Earth Scenes/OSF/Kathy Atkinson, p. 39; Animals Animals–Earth Scenes/Paddy Ryan, p. 41; AP Photo/Charlie Riedel, p. 43; AP Photo/Key/Janet Hostetter, p. 44; Big Stock Photo/Steve Lovegrove, p. 1; Big Stock Photo/Maria Dryfhout, p. 9; Big Stock Photo/John Pitcher, p. 15; Getty Images/George Grall/National Geographic, p. 8; Getty Images/Ross Land, p. 45; iStockphoto/Nick Berrisford, p. 32 (top); iStockphoto/Sergey Dubrovskiy, p. 31; iStockphoto/Bernard Johnson, p. 32 (bottom); Shutterpoint Photography/Robert Paulson, p. 28; Shutterpoint Photography/Armando Gasse, p. 29; Visuals Unlimited/Leonard Lee Rue III, p. 4.

Contents

Chapter 1 Fight to the Finish

Fight or flight? Some animals have to decide that every day. Most times, an animal will choose flight. They will try to run away or hide. It is a much safer choice. Some use their camouflage to hide, by blending in with their surroundings. Others copy the behavior or colors of dangerous animals.

There are times, however, that an animal has no choice but to stand its ground and fight. Every day, many animals have to fight for their

A mountain lion uses its weapons to get food. An unarmed hare is no match for sharp teeth and claws.

lives. It is an animal-eat-animal world out there! Having the right weapons is very important for survival. Many animals have weapons built right into their bodies. They may have sharp, spiky skin or hair. They may have long horns or tough hooves. Whatever weapon they have, these animals will use it if they have to.

Animals will often put on a show first. They will make a lot of noise. Animals may display their weapons to a predator. Sometimes, if a predator sees that an animal is able to fight back, it will not attack. These threats do not always work. That is when an animal might be forced to use its weapon. Using weapons for defense, however, can be risky.

One problem is that many predators have weapons of their own. They may be armed with sharp teeth and claws. Those powerful weapons can be very hard to defend against. To use a weapon for defense, an animal must be very

Prey animals can fight back if they have weapons. A water buffalo uses its sharp horns.

close to its predator. Obviously, being close to an animal that wants to eat you is not safe.

Many animals have special weapons to help with these problems. One of those special defenses is a spiky body. Spikes or spines are special hard hairs or skin. They cover an animal's body and stick up all over. If a predator cannot put its mouth around the animal, it usually cannot eat it. There are other defensive weapons as well.

Why Weapons?

There are many reasons that an animal uses physical weapons. Defense is just one of them. Many animals are predators who use weapons to get food. Animals with sharp claws can slash at their prey. Strong jaws and sharp teeth help in their attacks. Usually these animals rely on large size and speed also.

Many predators' weapons also deliver poison. The fangs of a venomous snake are a good example. Long, sharp fangs are a scary weapon by themselves. Some of them are powerful and sharp enough to pierce the toughest skin. A snake's bite and the venom it delivers can be a deadly combination.

There is one big difference between predators' weapons and weapons used only for defense. Predators' weapons are meant to kill.

Wild FACT

Male platypuses have spurs on their back legs that are poisonous. They use these weapons to fight other male platypuses. The poisonous spurs can also be used for defense against predators.

Shocking but True!

One of the wildest animal weapons is electricity! From a young age, humans are taught to leave electricity alone. We know how dangerous it can be. But some animals come with their own high-voltage weapon system. Electric eels have a built-in version of a stun gun. They use electricity to protect themselves. They also use it to catch food.

An electric eel is not really an eel at all. It is a snakelike fish. It has three special organs in its body. These organs can produce a dangerous electric shock. The electric eel can create different levels of electricity. It is almost completely blind. So, it uses low-level electric shocks to figure out where it is swimming.

When the electric eel senses danger or finds food, however, the real sparks start. The electric eel can create an electric shock up to 600 volts. That is about five times more electricity than comes out of an outlet in a home—and the electricity in a home outlet is enough to seriously injure or kill a person. This big shock helps keep predators from turning the eel into a meal.

A rattlesnake uses its weapons for defense. This predator's fangs and deadly venom can also kill.

These weapons are deadly. On the other hand, weapons for protection are usually designed to cause injury or pain—not death. Their purpose is to give an animal in danger some time to get away.

Next to eating, having babies is one of the most important things in any animal's life. Many male animals will use any weapon they have to fight for a female. They will use horns

Animals use their weapons against their own species, but not usually to cause death. Zebras fight with their hooves

or hooves. They will use tusks or teeth. These fights can last for hours. They can result in serious injuries. It is rarely a fight to the death though. One male will often simply give up and go away. The winner is the male that best uses his weapons. He is the one that gets the female.

Animals also fight each other for territory. Having enough room to live, eat, and raise young is very important to an animal's survival.

Many will defend their territories fiercely. Any animal that comes near the home or hunting grounds of another animal better be ready for a big fight.

Dee-fense!

One thing many animals will use their weapons for is to defend their young. A young animal often does not have any way to protect itself. Its weapons may not be fully developed, or it might not know just what to do with them until it is older. Some wild animal babies rely on their parents to protect them. From predator animals to prey animals, adults will often fight to the death for their babies.

Sometimes, however, the best way to win a fight is not

Some animals will fight to the death to defend their young.

by attacking, but by defending. Playing defense is tough, though. It is not always easy to guess what a predator is going to do when it attacks. A prey animal has to be ready for anything.

WILD FACT **Giraffes have very few natural predators. They do, however, fight each other, often for living space or over females. Male giraffes use their long necks and big heads as weapons. They whack each other over and over.**

No defense is perfect. Even the best weapons can sometimes be defeated. Many predators have learned how to get around some animal weapons. For example, some predators have learned how to crack open an animal's protective shell. Others have learned how to attack only the unprotected parts of their prey's body. For the most part, however, wicked weapons do the trick.

Getting a Leg Up on the Enemy

Some animals use their feet and legs as weapons. The kangaroo and zebra are two animals that will kick to defend themselves. Few animals, however, pack as big a punch for their size as the weta. What is a weta? It is a huge insect that lives in New Zealand. It looks very similar to a giant grasshopper. There are several types of weta. Most of them are gentle. The tree weta, however, can be quite a kicker.

When threatened, this weird bug will raise its back legs high in the air. Just like most animals, the tree weta's goal is to scare off a predator with this display. If the attacker keeps coming, the tree weta will kick with its long back legs. The kick itself does not hurt. The many spines along its back legs do, however. They can cause a nasty scratch to the predator that could become infected.

13

Chapter 2   Sticklers for Safety

The porcupine is one of the best-armed animals in the world. It has thousands of sharp quills all over its body. These prickly quills are a good weapon against predators. They can cause very serious injury to any animal who tries to attack a porcupine.

The quills of all porcupines are really special hairs. When a baby porcupine is born, its quills are very soft. They quickly harden. In fact, it takes less than an hour for the baby's

Porcupines are nocturnal, meaning they come out at night. They need good weapons to stay safe.

quills to become weapons. The quills grow just like any other hair. They will keep growing throughout the porcupine's life.

When a porcupine's quills get too long, they break off at the base. Sometimes they break off during a battle with another animal. There are always new quills growing to replace any that are lost. The porcupine is never without its weapons.

Shake, Rattle, and Roll

Porcupines are very shy animals. They are usually nocturnal. This means they are active mostly at night, while they sleep during the day. It is when the porcupine

Soon after birth, a baby porcupine's soft quills turn into hard, prickly weapons.

is out in the open and looking for food that it is in the most danger of being attacked by predators.

Normally, a porcupine's quills lie flat against its body. They are put into action only when the porcupine is threatened. Then, special muscles in the porcupine's skin raise all of the quills up straight. (The same muscles in humans' skin cause goose bumps.) A porcupine does not use its quills right away. It usually tries to scare a predator off first by making all kinds of noise.

Wild FACT The crested porcupine of North Africa is the largest type of porcupine in the world. Some of its quills can be more than a foot long!

Some kinds of porcupine have special quills on their tail. These tail quills are not solid. They are hollow. When a porcupine shakes these quills, they knock against each

When a lion gets too close, a porcupine turns around, ready to give it a face full of quills.

other. This makes a rattling sound to scare off predators.

If shaking its quills to frighten off the predator does not work, the porcupine then turns its back to the enemy. Quills always point backward. By turning around, the porcupine prepares its weapons. It also protects its head from an attack.

A porcupine will often scoot backward toward the enemy. If the animal still attacks,

Using Their Heads!

Many animals come equipped with huge weapons on their heads. They are horns and antlers. These weapons come in many different shapes and sizes. Some are long and straight. Others are curly. Still others branch out in every direction. Whatever they look like, horns and antlers can do major damage to an attacking animal.

There is a difference between horns and antlers. Horns are made of keratin. That is the same material  that hair, fingernails, and hooves are made of. Horns grow out of a bony plate in an animal's head. They keep growing as the animal gets older. Antlers, on the other hand, are made of bone. They do not keep growing. Each year, the antlers fall off and the animal grows a new pair.

Animals can use these horns or antlers as spears. They can also use them to deliver a big head-butt. This is a pretty good defense against a predator.

they are met with a face full of sharp quills as the porcupine backs into the attacker. The quills stick inside the animal's skin. Then they break off from the porcupine. The pain of a face full of quills distracts and stuns the predator. This gives the porcupine enough time to get away from its attacker.

Tiny barbs cover the surface around the end of each quill. These barbs face in the opposite direction from the quill point. This makes the quills very hard to remove. When an animal pulls at the quill stuck in its skin, the barbs push the opposite way. Ouch!

The Flip Side

A prickly coat and a plan of defense does not mean the porcupine is out of danger. In Africa, lions and hyenas love to eat porcupines. In North America, a weasel-like animal called the fisher has porcupine on its menu. These animals have figured out the porcupine's one weak spot.

It is possible for a predator to win a fight with a porcupine. But it will probably take home some painful souvenirs.

There are no quills on a porcupine's belly. It is soft, furry, and completely unprotected. Many predators have learned to flip porcupines over to attack them. It is not as easy as it may seem. These animals still have to fight an arsenal of pointy prickles to flip over the porcupine. Some animals walk away with a few quills stuck in them even if they win the fight!

Open Wide and Say Ahhhhh!

Some animals, such as warthogs, elephants, and walruses, have special teeth called tusks. Animals do not use their tusks for eating. They are far too long for chewing.

Tusks are most often used as tools. Animals with tusks can use them to lift things or to dig with. A walrus even uses its huge tusks to help move itself around.

Males use their tusks as swords. They often fight each other over females or land. Animals can also use these weapons for defense. Predators think twice before getting into a fight with any animals armed with large tusks.

Chapter 3   Hairy Little Ninjas

Tarantulas look pretty scary. Some can be as big as an adult's hand. They have two huge fangs that terrify many humans. Those fangs, however, are not used as a first line of defense. They are usually used only for getting food. Instead, when it is threatened, the tarantula does its best ninja impression. But instead of throwing Chinese stars, this spider throws hairs!

A tarantula's most important defensive weapons are the hairs that cover its body.

Tarantulas are different from other spiders. They have jaws that open up and down. Other spiders have jaws that open from side to side. Then, of course, there is all that hair. The tarantula's body is covered with thousands of tiny hairs.

Wild FACT

Tarantulas got their name in Taranto, Italy. In the 1300s dancing was against the law there. As the legend goes, people made up a dance called the "tarantella." They claimed that the reason they were jumping around so much was because they had been bitten by spiders. This kept them from getting in trouble with the law.

Hair, There, and Everywhere

A tarantula's hairs are very important. They help the spider feel vibrations. When another animal walks, hops, or flies nearby, it causes

Fangs a Lot!

When a tarantula feels food wandering nearby, it rises up on its back legs. Then the spider pounces on the animal with its two huge fangs.

The fangs inject venom into the prey. This does two things. First, the venom paralyzes the animal so it cannot move. Next, the venom turns the animal's insides into liquid. Tarantulas cannot chew. They have to drink their meals. This sounds scary, but no tarantulas are actually dangerous to humans. Their bite feels more like a wasp sting. In fact, many people keep tarantulas as harmless pets—fangs and all!

small vibrations. The hairs on the spider's body feel these movements. This lets the spider know exactly where lunch might be. The tarantula is also in danger of becoming lunch itself. Animals such as weasels, skunks, snakes, owls, and other large birds sometimes catch and eat tarantulas.

When the tarantula feels threatened, it uses its hairs in a whole other way. It throws them at its attacker. The hairs suddenly become weapons. Like most animals, the

Wild FACT
The biggest spider in the world is the goliath birdeater tarantula. Stretched from leg to leg, it can be more than a foot long!

tarantula does not fight at first. It often stands up tall on its back legs. It shows its fangs to its enemy. The spider hopes this bluff will work to scare the other animal away.

This big show does not always work. If it does not, the tarantula whips out a ninja move. It turns around and backs toward the attacker, using its rear legs to fling hairs off its back. That might not sound too threatening, but these

Undercover Sting Operation

Many people have accidentally met the weapon end of a wasp. Both wasps and bees can leave a painful sting when they feel they are in danger. Bees can die after a sting. They use their stingers only if their other defenses do not work. Wasps, on the other hand, can defend themselves much more aggressively.

A wasp is an insect. It has three body parts: a head, a thorax, and an abdomen. The stinger is located at the end of the abdomen (below). Wasps use their stingers to capture food, in addition to using them as defensive weapons.

Attached to the stinger is a venom gland. When the wasp stings an attacker, a tiny amount of the venom is released through the stinger. Many people and animals are very allergic to bee or wasp venom. It can cause terrible swelling and pain. Some stings can even cause death.

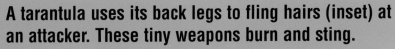

A tarantula uses its back legs to fling hairs (inset) at an attacker. These tiny weapons burn and sting.

tiny hairs can cause quite a bit of pain. Each little hair is covered with even tinier barbs on the end. These barbs help the hair stick in the enemy's skin.

The tiny weapons can cause bad itching and burning for the unfortunate animal that encounters them. Sometimes it can last for days. The predator forgets about the spider. It is too focused on the painful hairs. This gives the tarantula plenty of time to run to safety.

27

Chapter 4   Aquatic Arsenals

The ocean can be a dangerous place. It can be especially hard on slow-moving animals. That is why the sea urchin has such great weapons. Its entire body is covered with sharp spikes, or spines. This makes the sea urchin look like a pincushion!

The spiky sea urchin has many predators. They include its cousin, the starfish.

Sea urchins are in the same animal group as starfish. They are both called echinoderms (a-KINE-a-derms). That is a Greek word meaning "spiny skinned." Sea urchins are the spiniest of all echinoderms. They are protected with an arsenal of spikes. Sometimes, the spikes are even poisonous. They are attached to a hard, chalky covering called a test. The test covers and protects the round, soft body of the sea urchin.

Sea urchin spikes come in all lengths: short, very long like these, or somewhere in the middle.

Most sea urchins live in salty, shallow waters. They can live in oceans all over the world. Some even live in deeper waters. They eat mostly algae, which are small plant-like organisms that live in the water. Sea urchins also eat tiny bits of plants or animals they find on the ocean floor. But sometimes when a sea urchin is looking for food it finds itself on the menu. Many animals love to eat them!

Wild FACT No place is safe for a sea urchin. They even have predators on land. Many people love to eat sea urchins. In Japan, they are seen as a delicious treat.

Sea otters, for example, like to dive for sea urchins. When they find one, the otters smash them open for a tasty snack. The sea urchin is not even safe from its cousin, the starfish. But predators do not just come from the ocean. The sea urchin has enemies in the air also—many ocean birds eat sea urchins.

Many animals find sea urchins a tasty treat. But their spines make them very hard to eat.

The soft body parts inside the sea urchin's tough outer covering is what animals want to eat. But it is not as easy as it might seem. An animal that wants sea urchin for a meal has to do battle with the urchin's spiny body.

All Puffed Up

One type of fish uses spines as weapons also. The pufferfish can change its shape when threatened. Normally, it swims along and looks like any other fish (top). Its spines lie flat against its side. These spines are really special scales on the fish's body. When a predator attacks a pufferfish, the pufferfish gulps

water into its body. As its body becomes round, its spines pop up (bottom). They stick out everywhere. The pufferfish looks like a big, spiky ball!

This helps the pufferfish in two ways. First, puffing up makes it too big to swallow. Second, the spiky skin can hurt the predator. Some types of pufferfish, such as the fugu, have more deadly defenses. The fugu has very poisonous internal organs. Eating it would be deadly for any animal. In Japan, these pufferfish are a treat for some people even though eating them can be dangerous. In fact, nearly 50 people die in Japan each year from eating fugu.

A sea urchin has tiny claws all over its body. They are a backup weapon, as well as a way to catch food such as this shrimp (in the center).

A Prickly Situation

There are more than 900 different kinds of sea urchins. They come in a wide variety of colors and sizes. Their spines can be very different also. Most sea urchins have sharp, pointed spines. They can be long, short, or in between. These sharp spines often break off when the

Steady the Harpoon!

Sting rays carry their weapons on their tail. These animals are related to sharks. Their skeletons are not made of bone. Instead, they are made of cartilage. This is the same bendable material that human ears are made of.

Sting rays are usually peaceful creatures. They glide along the ocean floor looking for food. When they sense a threat, however, they launch their weapons. On their tail is a hard spike. It is almost like a spear. The sting ray whips its tail around to stab the predator with the sharp spike.

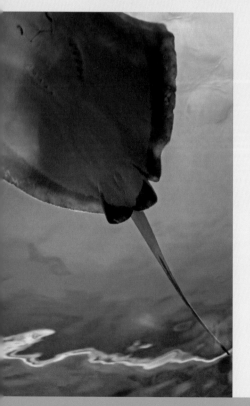

Near the tail spike are venom glands. These release poison along with the stab from the sting ray's tail. If the sting ray is attacked and cannot escape, it lashes out with its tail. The hard, sharp spike itself can cause a nasty wound. Then the poison causes a painful sting. These two things together are enough to give the sting ray a chance to get away from a predator.

sea urchin is attacked. They can stick in the skin of a predator and cause a nasty wound. Many of the pointy sea urchins have spines that are poisonous.

Wild FACT A sand dollar is a close cousin of the sea urchin. Its spines are very tiny. They make the sand dollar look more fuzzy than spiky.

Sea urchins also have a backup defense. In between their spines are tiny claws. These tiny pincers help keep the sea urchin clean. They help find and grab food. The tiny pincers can also be poisonous just like the spines. If some animal manages to defeat the sea urchin's spines, the pincers are there as a second defense.

Chapter 5

Devilish Defenses

When it comes to defenses, the thorny devil has it all. Its skin is colored to blend in with its desert environment, and it can change colors depending on the type of ground it is on, to blend in even better. It also has a "false head," which is really a fatty lump on the thorny devil's neck. It tricks predators into attacking the false

The thorny devil is a master of defense. The "thorns" on its body make most predators stay away.

head while the thorny devil's real head stays protected. Next, the thorny devil can puff up to look large and scary. And as if all that were not enough, it is covered in . . . well, thorns!

The thorny devil is a type of spiny lizard. It lives only in the sandy desert areas of Australia. Despite its scary name, the thorny devil is not very big. It is only about six inches long.

During warm days, it hunts for ants. Thorny devils eat ants and only ants. They are fast eaters. Thorny devils have been known to eat up to 45 ants a minute!

But this is the only thing about the thorny devil that is fast. In fact, it is a very slow-moving lizard. Because it is so slow, it needs

WILD FACT The thorny devil is also called a Moloch. Scientists who discovered the lizard in the 1800s named it Moloch after a terrible, violent demon character in a famous 17th-century book called *Paradise Lost* by John Milton.

all of its defenses for protection. Many animals try to eat the thorny devil despite its spiky skin. Large birds called bustards and even lizards called goannas hunt for thorny devils.

Wild FACT Female thorny devils lay between three and ten eggs each year. The babies are already fully armed with spikes when they hatch.

Making a Point

Unlike many animals, the thorny devil does not run away when threatened. It is just not fast enough to get away. Instead, the thorny devil stands its ground. It relies on its many defenses for protection. Changing color is one trick. The thorny devil's brownish color helps it blend in with the sandy Australian deserts. But it can also change to different shades of brown, red, and yellow to blend in with whatever color sand it happens to be walking on at the time.

To try to scare away a predator, a thorny devil puffs itself up with air to appear larger than it is.

If that does not work, and the thorny devil is spotted by a predator, it puffs itself up with air. This makes it seem bigger and scarier than it really is. This defense bluff sometimes works and scares off a predator. But not always. Next on the list of the thorny devil's defenses is a false head.

On the back of the thorny devil's spiky neck is a large bulge also covered in spikes. The thorny devil will duck its head and lift this

Seeing Red!

The horned lizard is a distant cousin of the thorny devil. Horned lizards are found in the southwestern United States and in parts of Mexico. These spiky little lizards are also sometimes called "horny toads." But they are not toads at all. Some types of horned lizard also have one of the weirdest defenses of any animal in the world. When attacked, horned lizards shoot blood out of their eyes!

When it senses danger, the horned lizard's brain signals blood vessels near its eyes to break.

Special ducts let some horned lizards shoot up to one-third of the blood in their body. They can shoot it more than three feet at a predator.

This weird weapon confuses and frightens a predator. That gives the horned lizard enough time to get away. As in all creatures, the horned lizard's body is always making new blood cells. The lost blood will slowly be replaced.

fatty area. Animals might think this is the thorny devil's head. They will be tempted to attack this area. The thorny devil's real head stays protected. It might be able to get away.

Not many predators will take on an animal whose whole body looks like a weapon!

What the thorny devil really counts on, however, are the sharp, pointy spikes on its skin. These spikes are where the thorny devil gets its name. The spikes are not poisonous. But they do make the thorny devil very hard to eat. So, most snakes and larger lizards leave the thorny devil alone.

Living to Fight Another Day

While most animals will always choose to flee danger when they can, the lucky few with weapons can stand and fight. Some use horns

41

or hooves. Others rely on prickly spines, spikes, or quills. A few even have poison as a backup defense. Animals with weapons at least have a fighting chance against predators.

Only the animals with the best weapons will survive. No matter which one an animal uses, its wicked weapons are truly an amazing animal defense.

Wet Weaponry

The pointy spikes of the thorny devil are great weapons. They are also very important in other ways. For example, the spikes even help the thorny devil get water. The deserts of Australia are very dry. Little rain falls there. In many places, there is as little as four inches of rain in a year. This means that drinking water is hard for animals to find.

The thorny devil's spikes form a system of grooves along the lizard's back. Any water that falls on the thorny devil's back travels down these grooves. The grooves lead down to the thorny devil's mouth for a welcome drink.

Police officers have learned a thing or two from animal weapons. They risk their lives every day to keep people safe. The police need great defenses in order to do their job well.

While most police officers are armed with guns to protect people against criminals, they have other, less deadly things they can use as well. Police always try to use these nonlethal weapons first. This means that the weapons do not cause death. These kinds of weapons help stop criminals without killing them. Most animals have nonlethal defensive weapons also.

One nonlethal weapon that police can use to stop a criminal is a taser. Tasers are electric stun

A nonlethal weapon called a sting ball grenade is launched at a target during a military exercise.

43

guns that can be fired from a short distance. The taser delivers an electric charge, much like the system that the electric eel uses. A taser's electrical charge is around 50,000 volts. The shock you get from walking across a rug and touching a doorknob, called static electricity, can be around 20,000 volts. By comparison, a lightning strike has around 300 million volts!

The electrical charge from the taser works to disrupt the messages sent by the body's nervous system. The taser gives just enough of a jolt to stop a person, but not enough to kill. Nevertheless, it can be dangerous and should never be handled by anyone not trained to use it. Once in a while, there are deadly results from the use of a taser. Since the electrical shock disrupts nervous system messages, the heart can be affected. The shock may affect the rhythm of the heart, or stop it completely. This is rare, however.

The police have learned another good trick from animals. Spikes can stop bad guys! They are a great defensive weapon. Many times, criminals get into a car chase with the police. Driving at such fast speeds is very dangerous for everyone. Police have to try to stop the criminal without causing a bad wreck.

The best way to stop a speeding car is with spike strips. These strips are topped with short metal spikes. Police officers lay the spike strips along the road (see bottom of photo). When the criminal speeds over the strip, the tires are popped. It is not long before the car has to stop and police can arrest the criminal.

Glossary

barbs—Sharp points that face in the opposite direction from a main point.

camouflage—When an animal uses its appearance or color to blend in with its surroundings.

cartilage—Tough, bendable tissue in the body. (Ears are made of cartilage.)

defense—Protection against an attack.

echinoderms—A group of ocean animals identified by their spiny skin.

keratin—A tough material that makes up hair, fingernails, hooves, feathers, and horns.

nonlethal—Something that will not cause death.

paralyze—To make unable to move.

predator—An animal that hunts and eats other animals.

prey—Any animal that is a food source for other animals.

territory—The area in which an animal lives.

Further Reading

Books

Jango-Cohen, Judith. *Porcupines*. Tarrytown, N.Y.: Benchmark Books, 2005.

Montgomery, Sy. *The Tarantula Scientist*. Boston: Houghton Mifflin, 2004.

Rhodes, Mary Jo. *Survival Secrets of Sea Animals*. Danbury, Conn.: Children's Press, 2007.

Trueit, Trudi Strain. *Lizard*. Danbury, Conn.: Franklin Watts, 2003.

Internet Addresses

National Geographic: Tarantulas
http://www.nationalgeographic.com/tarantulas/index2.html

Outback Australia Travel Guide:
The Thorny Devil Lizard
http://www.outback-australia-travel-secrets.com/thorny-devil.html

PBS Kids: Kratt's Creatures
http://pbskids.org/krattscreatures/login.shtml?

Sheppard Software: Porcupine
http://www.sheppardsoftware.com/content/animals/animals/mammals/porcupine.htm

Index